# How to tie
## 25
### tie
### essential
### knots

Mandy Clinnch

DROPSToNE PRESS
How to Tie 25 Essential Knots
Mandy Clinnch

Copyeditor: Jacob Perry
Photography: Mandy Clinnch
Photography: Makiyah Clinnch
Layout and Design: River Design Company

Published by DROPSToNE PRESS
978-1-947281-14-1

DROPSToNE
— P R E S S —
dropstonepress.com

# Introduction

Have you ever wanted to learn how to tie knots, but it seemed too difficult? It's my hope that this book will change all of that. I've broken down 25 fundamental knots with clear instructions and an image for each step in the tying process. To really understand a knot, you need to see it at every stage, so you can fully grasp how it is formed. With patience and practice you'll be able to confidently pass this knowledge on to others. I recommend working on one knot at a time, until you have mastered it, before moving on to the next one. You'll find the knots in this book have been placed in alphabetical order, making it easy to find the one you want to work on.

Knots are often an overlooked part of our everyday life, but they really do play an important role. Most of us learned how to tie our shoes at an early age, and now we do so without even thinking about it. Humans have been tying knots since the beginning of time and evidence of this has been found on numerous archaeological digs. Over the years sailors have depended on and created a lot of the most prevalent knots seen today. Also, you might be surprised by the fact that knot tying isn't just a human skill. The hagfish will tie itself in knots to assist in eating their prey, and the Weaver Bird ties knots to form its nest.

In this book I will be teaching you 25 essential knots with step-by-steps instructions. I've chosen to use 550 parachute cord, which has a nylon (polyamide) sheath filled with seven inner strands. This is an incredibly useful material for a multitude of things, but in this book it's for teaching purposes only. You will want to make sure that you have the correct rope for the job before you use a knot for heavy duty tasks, such as rock climbing. I encourage you to practice with as many different types of rope as possible and learn which works best for your individual application.

# Table of Contents

# Table of Contents

# 1

# Alpine Butterfly

**(BUTTERFLY KNOT, BUTTERFLY LOOP, LINEMAN'S LOOP, LINEMAN'S RIDER)**

The Alpine Butterfly forms a fixed loop in the middle of a rope. The Alpine Butterfly Knot can be tied around your hand. It can also be tied in the opposite direction by reversing each step. It's a secure knot often used by climbers because it is easy to untie, even after bearing weight. One unique advantage that sets this knot apart from others is that it can be tied in the middle of a length of rope when the ends may not be accessible.

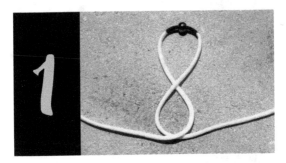

**Start by making two counter-clockwise twists**
(I've darkened the middle of the bight and added a silver bead so it will be easier to follow).

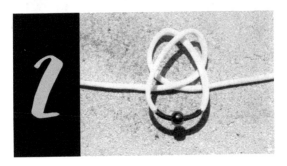

**Next, pull the top bight down and over the top of the bottom twist.**

Then, take the bight under and up
through the second twist.

Tighten knot to finish.

# 2

# Anchor Bend

## (FISHERMAN'S BEND)

Though it is a hitch, this knot is known as both the Anchor Bend and the Fisherman's Bend. It is known to be more secure than the Round Turn and Two Half Hitches, especially when using slippery rope. As the name suggests, this knot is great for securing a rope to an anchor point, such as a boat anchor.

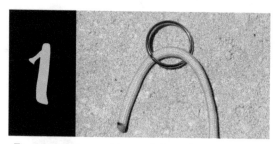

First, bring the working end through or around the object that you want to secure it to.

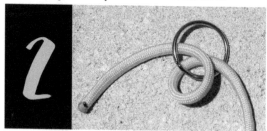

Wrap again either through or around the object, making a round turn.

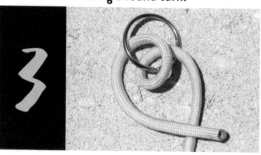

Cross the working end in front of the standing end.

Bring the working end through the round turn,
making a Half Hitch.

Dress the knot and add another Half Hitch.

Tighten to finish.

# 3

# Bowline

**(BOWLING, BOLIN, BOWLIN, BOLING)**

Often referred to as the King of Knots, the Bowline won't disappoint. As an ancient knot, it has withstood the test of time, and it is still widely used today. The purpose of this knot is to create a fixed loop at the end of a rope. This fixed loop is most reliable when under load, which makes it a great rescue knot.

**Start by making an overhand loop.**

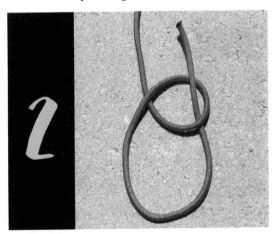

**Next, bring the working end under and up through the overhand loop.**

Pass the working end behind the standing end.

Then, bring the working end down through the overhand loop.

Pull on both ends to tighten.

The Bowline can be made as large or small as you need it to be.

# 4

## Clove Hitch

**(BUILDER'S KNOT)**

The Clove Hitch is a simple way to start a lot of different projects. Also called a Builder's Knot, the Clove Hitch is basically two Half Hitches in succession. Although not as secure as the Constrictor Knot, it is still very useful and popular.

**Start by bringing your working end around a fixed object, like a pole or branch.**

**Then, cross it over at a diagonal.**

Next, wrap the working end around.

Then, tuck it under itself.

Finally, pull everything tight.

# 5

# Constrictor Knot

## (GUNNER'S KNOT, WHIP KNOT)

The Constrictor Knot is much more secure than the Clove Hitch. In fact, sometimes it will need to be cut off because it jams so well. It seems to work best with smaller rope and can be used for a variety of jobs including (but not limited to) securing bags, bundling sticks together, temporarily binding the ends of a rope, clamping hoses, tying bundles of herbs together to dry, etc.

**Start by bringing your working end around a fixed object, like a pole or branch.**

**Then, cross it over at a diagonal.**

Next, bring the working end around and cross it in front of the standing end.

Bring it under the bottom loop.

Then, bring it under the top loop.

**6**

Pull on both ends to tighten.

# 6

# Cow Hitch

## (LARK'S HEAD, RING HITCH, LANYARD HITCH)

The Cow Hitch has too many names and applications to mention. It can be tied with either a bight or the end of a rope. Many projects are started with a Cow Hitch, such as nets, paracord bracelets, key chains, lanyards, necklaces, as well as attaching tags to luggage. If you pass the running end through the turns when you're done, it becomes the Pedigree Cow Hitch, which will make the standing part more secure.

Start by bringing your working end over and to the right of the object to which you're attaching your cord.

Next, cross the working end in front of the standing end.

Then, wrap it behind.

Bring the working end under the bight you just made.

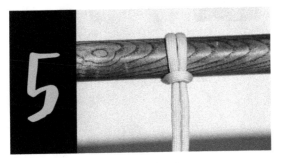

Pull tight to finish.

As a final option, when leaving a tag, you can take the working end through the turns to make a **Pedigree Cow Hitch**.

# 7

# Crown Knot

The Crown Knot is easy to learn, and a great way to start many projects, like pouches, plant hangers, and key chains. It can be fashioned spaced out as when making a net or close together to form a sinnet. You can tie the Crown Knot with three or more cords if being used for starting a Back Splice. In this case, I will be using two overlapping cords, which will result in four working ends for decorative work. Whether using three cords or four, always remember the final pattern will be: over, over, under, or—alternatively—over two, under one.

Cross two pieces of cord to make a "T" shape.

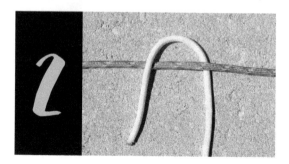

Bring the top vertical part straight down
over the left horizontal part.

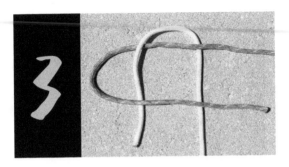

Next, bring the left horizontal part over
both vertical parts.

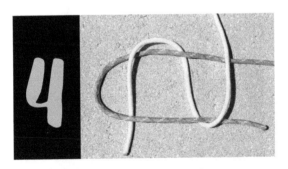

Then, bring the bottom vertical part up
over both horizontal parts.

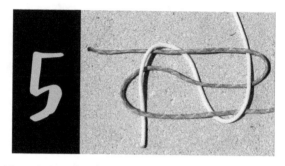

Next, bring the right horizontal part over the first two vertical parts and tuck it under the last. This leaves you with the pattern: over, over, under.

Pull on all four ends to tighten.

# 8

## Evenk Hitch

**(SIBERIAN HITCH, SLIPPED FIGURE OF EIGHT HITCH)**

The Evenk Hitch is an excellent "quick release" knot that would be beneficial for everyone to know. It can even be tied while wearing thick gloves, which makes it ideal for starting a tarp ridgeline in cold temperatures. The Evenk Hitch is an ideal anchor knot for many projects.

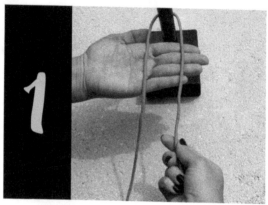

Start by bringing your working end around a tree or post, and lay it over your fingers.

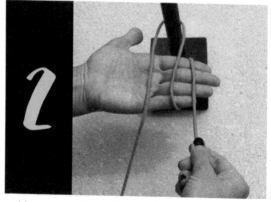

Next, wrap the working end around your hand.

Twist your hand under the standing end.

Bring your thumb through and make sure you have a twist in the cord or you'll end up making a Halter Hitch.

Pull a piece of the tag end through.

Finally, pull everything tight. For a quick release, simply pull the tag end of the rope and the knot will untie.

# 9

# Farrimond Friction Hitch

The Farrimond Friction Hitch hasn't been around for very long, but it has become one of my go-to "quick release" tension knots. It is easy to tie, easy to adjust, and even easier to untie. This friction hitch is ideal for drawing a rope tight between two points, such as when stringing a clothesline.

**Start by bringing the working end around your object.**

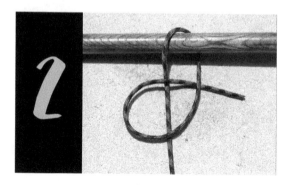

**Next, make an underhand loop and lay it over the standing end.**

Wrap the bight under the standing part.

Continue wrapping.

Then, make a second wrap and start dressing the knot.

Pull a bit of your tag end through the bight.

Finally, tighten everything up. You can now adjust the knot in either direction. Pulling on the tag end will release the entire knot all at once.

# 10
# Figure Eight Knot
(FIGURE OF EIGHT KNOT, SAVOY KNOT,
FLEMISH KNOT)

The Figure Eight is an amazing stopper knot that is easier to untie than an overhand knot. It is very recognizable, and the softly-tightened version is often used in decorative work because of its pretty shape. Rock Climbers and Sailors sometimes use it as a stopper knot in its fully-tightened form.

Cross the working end over the standing end.

Then, bring the working end under the standing end.

Next, bring the working end over and through the top loop.

Pull on both ends to form a decorative Figure Eight Knot.

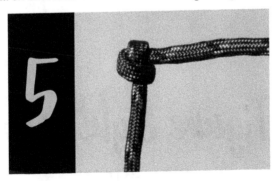

For a stopper knot, pull on the standing part while grasping the knot.

# 11

# Figure Eight Loop

### (FLEMISH LOOP)

While it is difficult to untie, the Figure Eight Loop is also easy to recognize. Seen a lot in climbing, it's a secure choice that can be made even stronger by attaching the working end to the standing end with an additional knot.

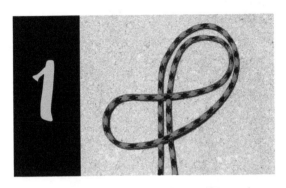

Form a bight and cross over the standing end.

Next, bring the working (bight) end under the standing part.

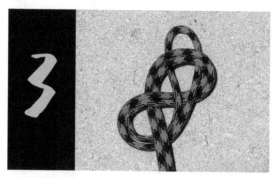

Then, bring the working end (bight) over and through the top loop.

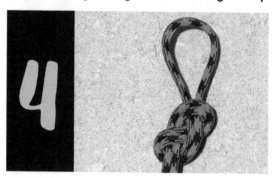

As you tighten you'll start to see the "8" begin to take shape.

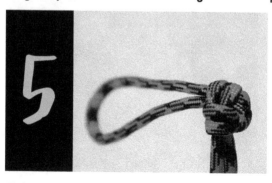

Pull on the knot and the standing end to tighten.

# 12

# Fisherman's Knot

## (WATERMAN'S KNOT, ANGLER'S KNOT, ENGLISHMAN'S KNOT)

This knot is ideal for securely joining the ends of two ropes together. The Fisherman's Knot is made by tying the working ends of two lines directly onto the standing parts of each other with overhand knots, thereby joining them together. You can also use one piece of cord to create a Fisherman's Knot when starting a Prusik Knot. The smaller the cordage used, the harder this bend is to untie. The Fisherman's knot is also good for making adjustable bracelets and necklaces.

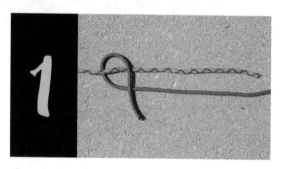

**Start by looping one working end over the other.**

**Then, form an Overhand Knot.**

Next, bring the other working end under that of the first.

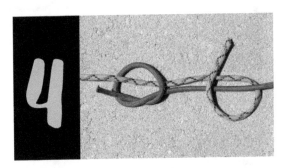

Loop it around.

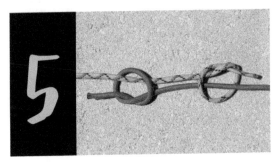

Create a second overhand knot.

Tighten both knots.

Lastly, slide them together to finish.

# 13

## Pile Hitch

The Pile Hitch is ideal for quickly setting up a perimeter. Attaching rope to a post is a breeze with this hitch, as it can be tied at any place in your line. It is traditionally tied in the bight as a temporary mooring hitch.

First, take the bight across your pole.

Next, bring it around and under the standing end.

Then, cross it over the standing end so that the bight can
come up and over the top of the pole.

Finally, slide down the pole and tighten.

# 14

## Rolling Hitch

The Rolling Hitch looks like the Clove Hitch. It is commonly used to attach a small rope to a larger rope. The standing end should be across the turns and pulled level with the rope or pole to which it is attached.

Wrap the working end around your object.

Then, cross over standing end and bring up to the top right.

Next, bring around and cross over the standing end again.

Then, bring around once more.

Tuck the working end back under itself.

Pull tight to finish.

# 15

# Round Turn and
# Two Half Hitches

Securing the end of a rope to a stationary object is easy with a Round Turn and Two Half Hitches. Its strength and reliability make it popular for mooring boats.

Start by bringing your working end around and to the left.

Then, wrap again to complete a round turn.

Next, bring the working end over and under the standing end to make the first Half Hitch.

Then, wrap again to make a second Half Hitch.

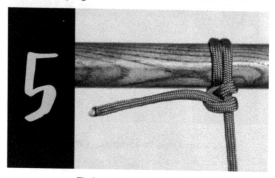

Tighten knot to finish.

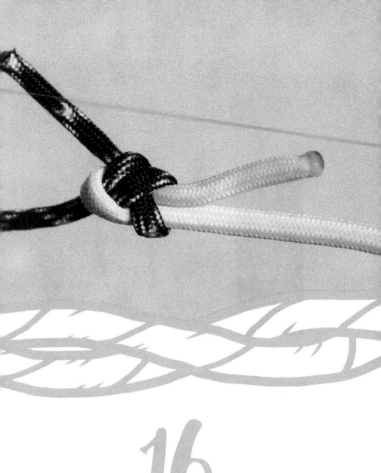

# 16
# Sansome Bend

The Sansome Bend is rarely used, but it is worth learning. It even works well on cord that is stretchy and slick. It's purpose is to join the ends of two lengths of rope. It was allegedly first used to attach two pieces of elastic to each other.

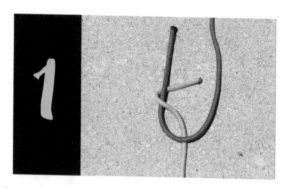

Start by bringing one cord under the other and wrap it around the working end of the second cord.

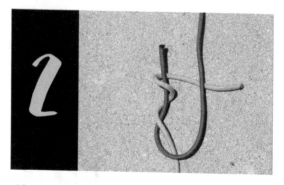

Next, wrap again around both parts of cord two.

Then, bring the working end down through itself two times.

Finally, tighten knot and make sure that both working ends are on the same side.

# 17
## Sheet Bend

**(BECKET BEND, FLAG BEND, COMMON BEND)**

This bend is structured like a Bowline, and it is great for joining two cords of different sizes. Start by forming a bight with the larger of the two cords and feed the smaller cord under and around the back of the bight. Then, finish by tucking it under itself. The Sheet Bend tends to loosen when it's not under load, and it doesn't provide a lot of strength. Thus, it shouldn't be used for heavy loads.

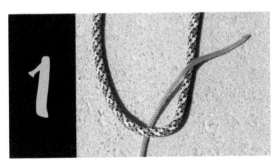

Start by bringing the smaller cord under the bight of the larger cord.

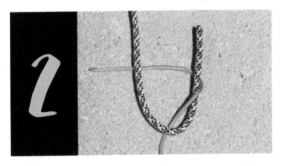

Then, take the smaller working end around the back of the bight.

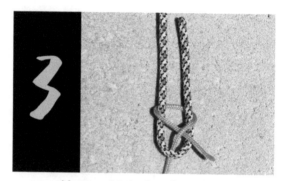

**Next, tuck it back under itself.**

**Tighten to finish.**

# 18

## Slipped Noose

A Slipped Noose is a quick and easy way to attach rope to a pole. It is also the beginning step to other knots, and it is used in knitting.

Begin by making a loop with the standing end on top.

Next, form a bight with the standing end, bringing it under and through the loop.

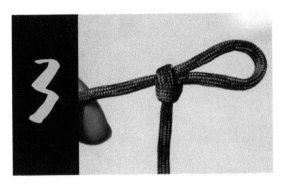

Tighten and adjust noose to the size needed for the
pole or stake to which you are attaching it.

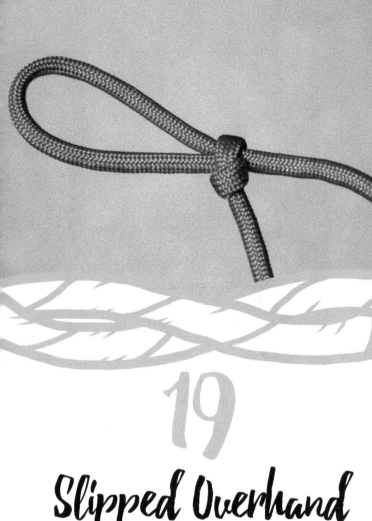

# 19
## Slipped Overhand Knot

A Slipped Overhand Knot can come in handy for many things. It is also the foundation for many other knots. It's simple to tie and comes undone by pulling on the working end. This is the knot most commonly used to tie shoes.

Start by making a loop with the working end on top.

Next, form a bight with the working end, bringing it under and through the loop. Make sure you leave enough of a tag end.

Tighten to finish.

# 20

# Square Knot

## (REEF KNOT)

The Square Knot will not be able to handle a heavy load when attaching two ropes together. It is a great way to tie parcels or decorations that will not require a lot of weight. It also works well for tying a jacket around your waist.

Start by crossing the working ends left over right.

Then, tuck it under.

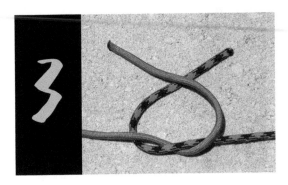

Next, cross right over left.

Tuck it under.

Pull on all four ends to tighten.

When you are finished, make sure that both
working ends are on the same side.

# 21

# Strangle Knot

First, bring the cord around object and to the right.

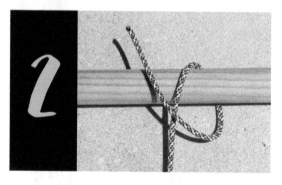

Then, cross over at a diagonal.

Next, bring the working end under the pole and
under the standing end.

Then, bring the working end back over the standing end.

Tuck the working end under the "X" of the turns.

Finally, pull on both ends to tighten.

# 22

# Surgeon's Knot

## (LIGATURE KNOT)

The Surgeon's Knot is a variation of the Square Knot, and it holds tension well without being bulky. It will work for joining any two pieces together, but it is mostly seen on smaller cord. It's no surprise that surgeons sometimes use this knot, since it binds even slippery lines quite well.

Start by crossing the right working end over the left.

Then, wrap around twice.

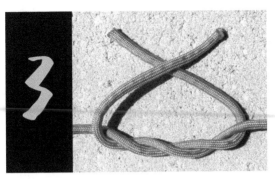

**3**

Next, cross left over right.

**4**

Wrap around once.

**5**

As you tighten, this knot will twist a bit.

# 23
## Taut Line Hitch

As far as adjustable tensioning knots go, most people have heard of the classic Taut Line Hitch. It is most often used to tension the guy lines for a tent, which makes it a convenient knot to know if you do a lot of camping.

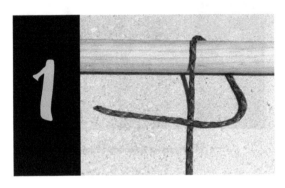

**Bring the working end around your stationary object and cross in front of the standing end.**

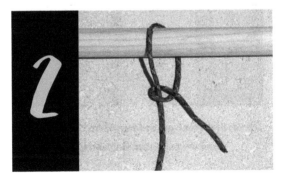

**Next, take the working end under the standing end.**

# 24

## Timber Hitch

The Timber Hitch can be used to drag heavy objects, such as logs. It creates a noose that holds if there is weight pulling on it. Once the weight is released, the knot is simple to undo.

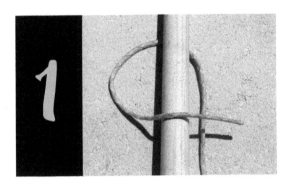

First, wrap the cord around your object and cross over standing end.

Then, bring the working end under the standing end and back over itself.

Next, wrap around three or more times.

Pull on standing end to tighten.

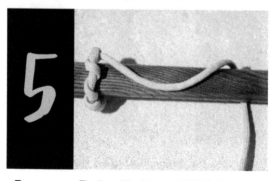

To turn your Timber Hitch into a Killick Hitch,
bring the standing end around the pole.

Then, bring it back under itself to make a half hitch.

Finally, pull on the standing end. This will assist in keeping anything you are dragging to stay level.

# 25

## Transom Knot

The Transom Knot shouldn't be used to replace the much stronger Square Lashing for a heavy job, but it can be very useful when you need a quick way to temporarily hold two intersecting pieces together for light duty jobs. You can add a second Transom Knot in the opposite direction to add strength. It is like the Constrictor Knot and structured like the Strangle Knot. It is great for light duty lashings with tent poles, garden structures, kites, etc.

Start by wrapping the working end around the back of the vertical post, but make sure it is above the horizontal post.

Next, cross the working end over the standing end with both pieces in front of the horizontal post.

Then, wrap the working end around the back of the vertical post. This time it needs to go below the horizontal post.

Bring the working end over the standing end, and under the bottom loop you created.

Then, bring it under the top loop.

Finally, pull both ends tight.

# Glossary

**The following knot terms are used in this book:**

*Standing End*   The end of the cord not being actively used to tie a knot. Opposite of the Working End.

*Working End*   The end of the cord being actively used to tie a knot. Opposite of the Standing End, also referred to as the "Tag End".

*Standing Part*   The middle section of cordage not being used between the standing and working ends.

*Bight*   Any part of the cord between the standing and working ends forming a doubled section that does not cross.

*Dressing the Knot*   Tightening the knot into its finished form by adjusting it in such a way as to shape correctly.

# Glossary

**Loop** Crossed section in between the standing and working ends.

**Overhand Loop** A loop where the working end is on the top of the standing part.

**Underhand Loop** A loop where the working end is on the bottom of the standing part.

**Stopper Knot** A knot tied at the end of the cord which results in a fixed point.

**Hitch** When a cord is tied to another object.

**Bend** When a cord or rope is tied to another cord or rope.

**Round Turn** To make a complete revolution around an object with the cord.

CPSIA information can be obtained
at www.ICGtesting.com
Printed in the USA
BVHW06s1931191018
530729BV00002B/2/P

9 781947 281141